Living for GOD

Living for GOD

James T. Dyet

REGULAR BAPTIST PRESS
1300 North Meacham Road
Schaumburg, Illinois 60173-4806

This study guide is one of seven
designed to be used with
Blueprint for Spiritual Maturity
from Regular Baptist Press.
Visit the Web site for further details.
www.regularbaptistpress.org/buildup

LIVING FOR GOD

Regular Baptist Press • Schaumburg, Illinois
www.regularbaptistpress.org • 1-800-727-4440
Printed in U.S.A.

RBP5335 • ISBN: 978-1-59402-315-6
Second Printing—2007

Contents

Preface

Because life is precious, we try to squeeze all we can out of it and put all we can into it. We exercise, eat sensibly (with the exception of overeating at church potlucks), try to sleep eight hours nightly, and schedule regular medical checkups. Some of us plan for retirement, hoping to live comfortably in our senior years. But the best life isn't simply one of good health, financial security, and comfort. The best life builds on the foundation of faith in Christ, honors God, and receives His approval. This kind of life makes every day enjoyable and significant.

The apostle Paul understood what the best life is all about. He declared, "For to me to live is Christ" (Philippians 1:21) and testified, "Christ liveth in me: and the life which I now live in the flesh I live by the faith of the Son of God, who loved me, and gave himself for me" (Galatians 2:20).

These lessons are dedicated to helping you live for God, grow in your relationship with Him, and experience victory over sin. This is the life God wants you to lead. You don't have to settle for less!

LESSON **1**

Living for God Starts with a Choice

"Choose you this day whom ye will serve; . . . but as for me and my house, we will serve the LORD" (Joshua 24:15).

Joshua, Israel's leader at the time of the conquest of Canaan, had turned 110. Knowing he did not have much longer to live, he offered his beloved nation, Israel, a final challenge to live for the Lord. He gathered Israel's tribes together at Shechem, rehearsed Israel's history, and commanded them to make a clear choice.

1. Read Joshua 24:1–13. Why couldn't Israel take credit for the nation's existence and survival?

2. Thinking back over your personal history, what has the Lord done for you that

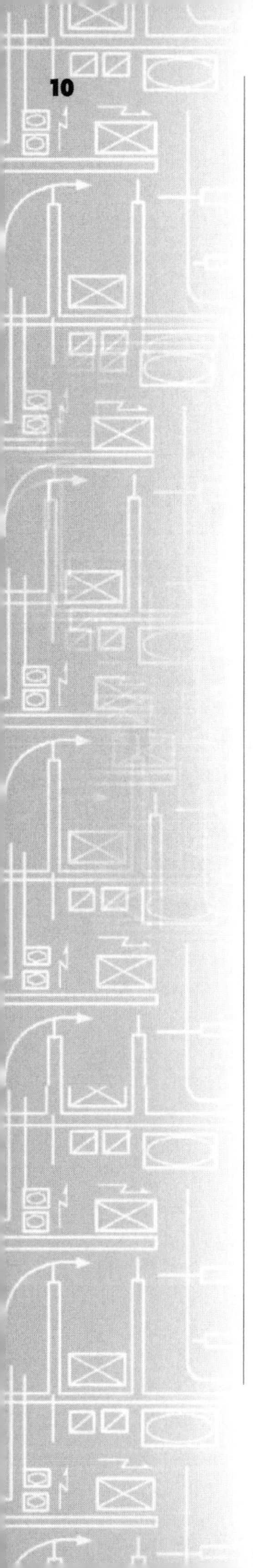

you could not have accomplished on your own?

ISRAEL'S CHOICE

The Lord had been good to Israel, and such kindness deserved an appropriate response. Joshua urged the Israelites to make a clear, firm choice between serving the false gods of the Canaanites and serving the Lord God of Israel (vv. 14, 15).

3. Read verse 24. What choice did the Israelites make?

CHOOSE TO FOLLOW CHRIST

When Jesus ministered on earth, He challenged people from many walks of life to follow Him. Each person had a choice: to pursue his own course or devote his life to Jesus. Simon (Peter), Andrew, James, and John made the all-important decision to follow Jesus after discovering firsthand that Jesus could do what seemed impossible.

The four men had fished all night, but not one fish had swum into their nets. They were washing the nets on the shore that memorable

morning when Jesus entered one of their boats and taught the people who lined the shore.

After "class," Jesus commanded Simon to "launch out into the deep, and let down your nets for a draught" (Luke 5:4). Would Simon choose to obey Jesus?

4. Read Luke 5:5–7.
   (a) What objection did Simon raise?

   (b) What choice did he make?

   (c) What did making this choice lead to?

Jesus offered Simon and the other fishermen another choice: to leave their fishing business and follow Him as fishers of men (v. 10). Would they walk away from the greatest catch of fish they had ever realized, knowing that the teeming nets represented abundant income? Would they follow Jesus?

5. Read Luke 5:11. What choice did the four men make?

Jesus doesn't call everyone to leave his or her occupation, but He does call every believer

To follow Jesus means to walk the same path He walked. His path is straight and narrow (Matthew 7:14), but it leads to joy, peace, significance, and eternal reward.

to follow Him. You may work as a plumber or a printer or a professor, but your primary calling is to follow Jesus as a godly believer. It is a choice you must make. Jesus said, "If any man serve me, let him follow me" (John 12:26).

CHOOSE TO ACKNOWLEDGE CHRIST AS LORD

Saul of Tarsus never expected to make a U-turn on the road to Damascus. He planned to go straight from Jerusalem to Damascus, arrest followers of Christ, chain them, and deliver them to Jerusalem for punishment. But something dramatic happened along the way. It turned his life around forever.

6. Read Acts 9:1–6.
   (a) Who appeared to Saul on the Damascus Road?

   (b) In your opinion, why was Saul "trembling and astonished"?

   (c) How did Saul show that he acknowledged Jesus as Lord?

Saul intended to arrest Jesus' followers in Damascus, but the risen Lord arrested him before he reached his destination. The Lord,

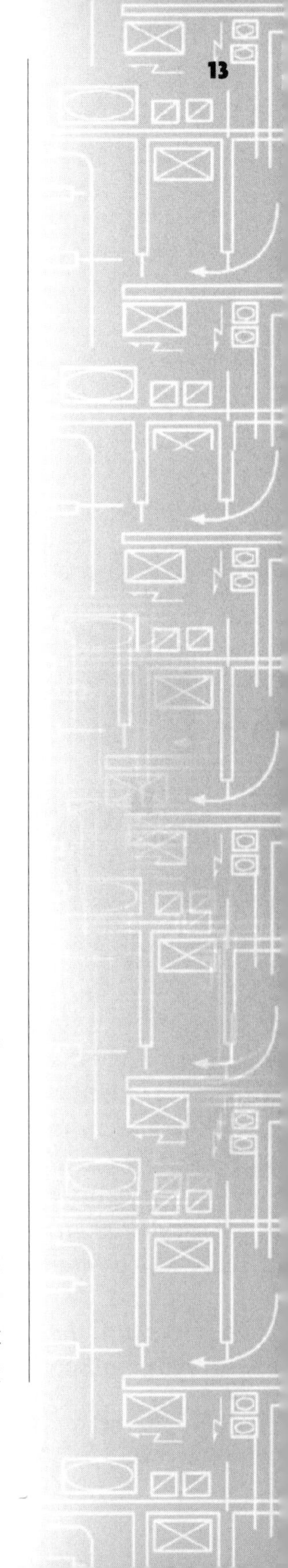

in Whom Saul placed his faith, appointed him an apostle to the Gentiles (Acts 9:15; Galatians 1:1; 1 Timothy 2:7). He became known as the apostle Paul, and he devoted the rest of his life to proclaiming the gospel on three continents.

7. How determined are you to follow the risen Son of God as your Lord?

8. What specific thing do you believe the Lord wants you to do for Him this week?

Paul learned quickly that living for God isn't easy. He encountered hostility similar to what he had hurled at believers before he trusted in Christ. Many Jews hated him and even tried to kill him. Sometimes Gentiles rioted against him when he preached in their cities. He narrowly escaped with his life when hateful Jews closed in on him at Damascus. Believers saved him by lowering him in a basket over the city's wall by night (Acts 9:23–25). At Lystra, Paul's Jewish persecutors persuaded residents to kill him. An angry mob stoned him, dragged him out of their city, and left him there, thinking he was dead (Acts 14:19). At Philippi, he and his coworker Silas were beaten and thrown into a jail's innermost cell, where stocks secured their feet. However, neither the beatings nor the confinement suppressed their joy. They filled the jail's dank midnight air with songs of praise to the Lord (Acts 16:24, 25).

In his second letter to the Corinthians, Paul listed the trials he had endured for the sake of the gospel. They included exhausting work, frequent incarceration, death-threatening episodes, lashings, beatings, stoning, shipwreck, the threat of drowning, constant dangerous travel in cities and open country, treacherous sea crossings, betrayals, weariness, pain, hunger, thirst, sleepless nights, food deprivation, exposure to cold, lack of sufficient clothing, and deep concern for the churches he had established (2 Corinthians 11:23–28).

But Paul had chosen to live for God, so he kept preaching the gospel. He committed himself to the task the Lord had given him, and nothing would prevent him from completing it.

Agrippa was the son of Herod Agrippa, who had beheaded the apostle James and imprisoned Peter (Acts 12:1–3). He was also the great-grandson

TESTIMONY BEFORE A KING

You might think that arraignment before a powerful ruler would dissuade Paul from his appointed task. But it didn't. The risen Lord had predicted that Paul would bear His name before kings (Acts 9:15), and sure enough Paul did so.

Acts 26 explains that Paul, a prisoner of the Roman Empire, stood before King Agrippa and recounted how the Lord had saved him and commissioned him to preach the gospel to the Gentiles. He testified, "Whereupon, O king Agrippa, I was not disobedient unto the heavenly vision. . . . Having therefore obtained help of God, I continue unto this day, witnessing both to small and great" (vv. 19, 22).

9. Which of Paul's trials do you think were the most severe?

10. What opposition and/or hardship might you have to endure as a consequence of living for God?

11. What motivates you to endure trials as a follower of Christ?

of Herod the Great, who had ordered the slaughter of all the male infants upon learning that Jesus had been born (Matthew 2:1, 16). He ruled territories northeast of Palestine on behalf of the Romans.

ULTIMATE JOY AND SERVICE

Later, when Paul was under a sentence of house arrest in Rome, he addressed a letter to the church at Philippi. Many Christians call Philippians the "Joy Epistle" because it contains so many references to joy and rejoicing. Even house arrest and the possibility of execution could not erase Paul's joy.

Years earlier Paul had chosen to live for God, a choice that gave him deep and permanent joy. His choice on the Damascus Road remained strong years later in Rome. He told the Philippians, "For to me to live is Christ, and to die is gain." He was determined to

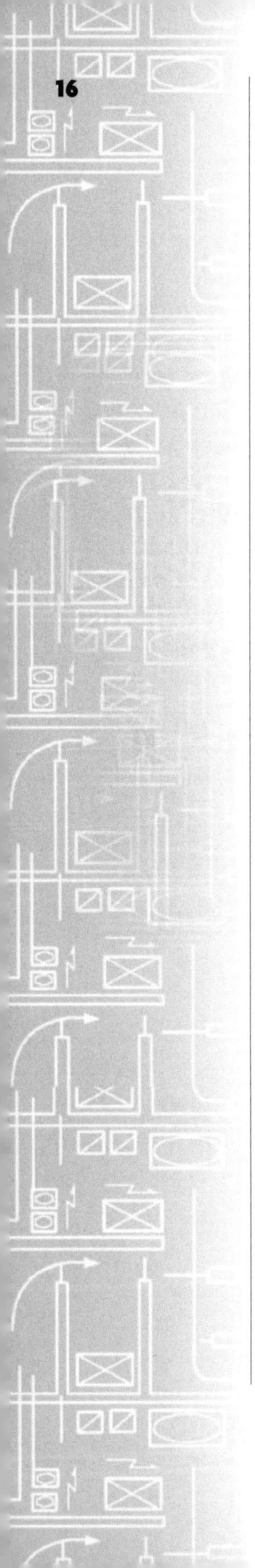

honor the Lord for the duration of his life. If an executioner's sword ended his life, he would die with an unwavering testimony.

While under house arrest, Paul seized every opportunity to live for God. He wrote the inspired New Testament letters of Ephesians, Philippians, Colossians, and Philemon. He also shared the gospel with the elite Roman soldiers who guarded him. As a result of his sterling life and witness, some of the guards trusted in Christ.

12. Read Philippians 1:13 and 4:22. How far did Paul's testimony for Christ reach?

FINISHING WELL

After his release from house arrest, Paul did not stop living for God. He continued to travel and preach the gospel until he was rearrested. This time he probably remained in a Roman prison until the authorities executed him.

Second Timothy, addressed to a young pastor, was Paul's last New Testament letter. Having lived for God throughout his Christian life, he offered wise counsel to Timothy. He urged him to flee "youthful lusts" and to follow "righteousness, faith, charity, peace, with them that call on the Lord out of a pure heart" (2 Timothy 2:22). He also emphasized the role of God's inspired Word in guiding the believer to spiritual maturity (3:16, 17).

As Paul neared the end of his life, he reflected on the life he had lived for God. In 2 Timothy 4:6 and 7 he wrote, "I am now ready to be offered, and the time of my departure is at hand. I have fought a good fight, I have finished my course, I have kept the faith." Living for God had not been easy, as the word "fight" suggests. The path of following the Lord had been long and arduous, not a sprint but a marathon. Nevertheless, every bout and every step had been worthwhile. Paul had lived for God's glory. He had led many people to Christ. Now he was about to meet the Lord and receive a victor's crown.

Paul penned these words in verse 8: "Henceforth there is laid up for me a crown of righteousness, which the Lord, the righteous judge, shall give me at that day." The Lord's approval would erase all the trials he had endured and lift all the burdens he had carried.

The word Paul used for "crown" is stephanos. *The* stephanos *was a laurel wreath awarded to victors at Greece's athletic games.*

Choosing to live for God is always the right choice!

FOR FURTHER THOUGHT

1. The apostle James described human life as "a vapour, that appeareth for a little time, and then vanisheth away" (James 4:14). However, life extends beyond death; and the Christian who chooses to live for God and does so realizes eternal significance. The apostle John wrote, "And the world passeth away, and the lust thereof: but he that doeth the will of God abideth for ever" (1 John 2:17).

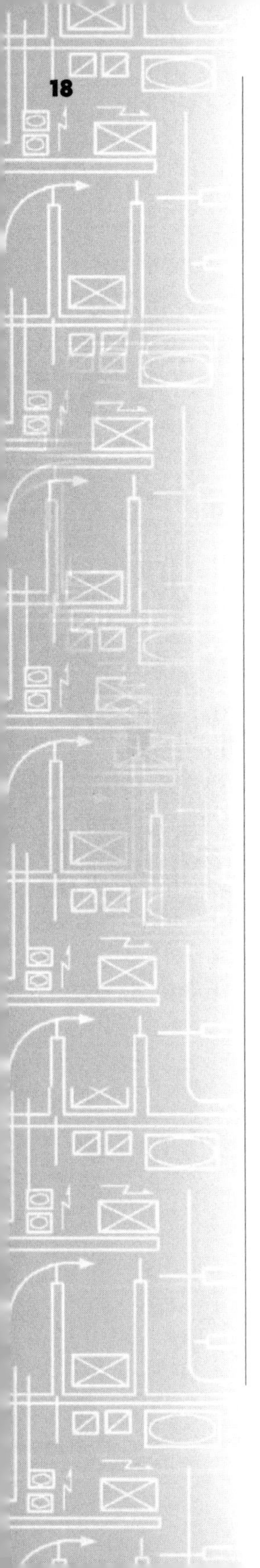

How does knowing life on earth is brief motivate you to live for God?

2. All who live for God influence their friends, family members, and fellow employees. Matthew 5:16 indicates that the goal of doing good works is to persuade others to glorify our Heavenly Father. If you live for God, what response do you expect to receive from your friends, family members, and fellow employees?

3. What do you think a believer loses if he chooses not to live for God? What does he gain if he chooses to live for God?

LESSON **2**

How Shall We Live?

"For the grace of God that bringeth salvation hath appeared to all men, teaching us that, denying ungodliness and worldly lusts, we should live soberly, righteously, and godly, in this present world" (Titus 2:11, 12).

Privilege brings responsibility. Proud parents smiling widely at their newborn baby girl or boy feel blessed and privileged. But major responsibilities accompany the privilege of welcoming a tiny baby into their hearts and home. The parents must feed, clothe, shelter, educate, and provide health needs for their child. Someday they may choose to take partial or even total responsibility for their son or daughter's college tuition. Wise parents begin early to put aside money for their daughter's wedding. Funding a wedding can be a huge responsibility.

When you believed on Jesus as your Savior, you were born into God's family. God, Who became your Heavenly Father, assumed responsibility for your care. Also, you were

The apostle John considered membership in God's family an astonishing privilege. He wrote, "Behold, what manner of love the Father hath bestowed upon us, that we should be called the sons of God" (1 John 3:1).

linked in this family to all true believers. They became your brothers and sisters in Christ with instructions from God to assume some responsibility for your spiritual development. So you are in good hands!

1. Read Matthew 6:30–33 and Philippians 4:19. What responsibility has your Heavenly Father assumed on your behalf?

2. Read Philippians 1:6 and 2:13. What further responsibility has your Heavenly Father taken on your behalf?

We do not respect a son or daughter who expects his family members to do everything for him. However, we do respect a child who assumes personal responsibility. After all, a productive person works hard to become a productive member of society. Similarly, each Christian must assume personal responsibility for his life. He needs to follow God's instructions, appropriate God's resources, and strive to live for God.

The apostle Paul's inspired letter to Titus, a pastor on the island of Crete in the Mediterranean Sea, brims with instructions on how to live for God. Cretans were infamous for their corrupt lifestyle and especially their lying. The

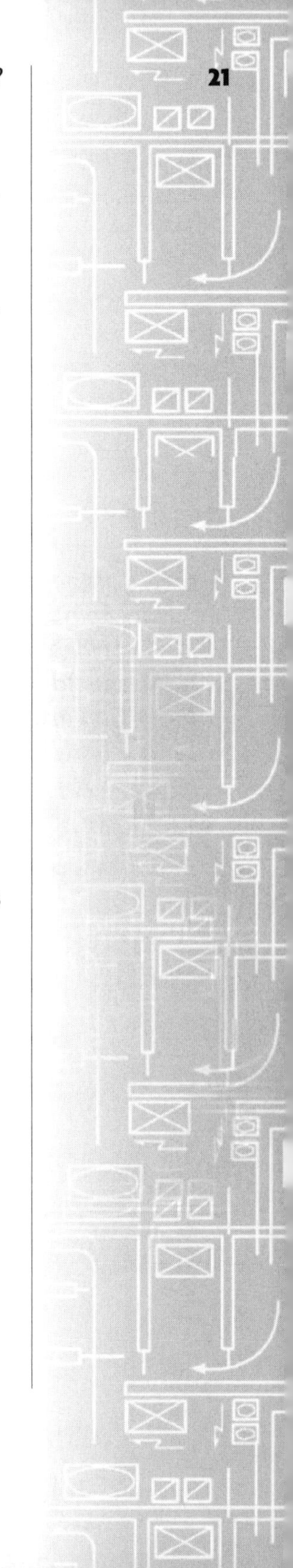

saved Cretans needed to show how thoroughly the gospel had changed their lives.

Paul's instructions helped the Cretans build a sterling reputation. Nestled in the middle of the letter to Titus is Paul's explanation that the grace of God that brings salvation also teaches us to renounce ungodliness and worldly lusts. But it also teaches us to live in three positive ways. We should live "soberly, righteously, and godly" (Titus 2:12).

LIVE SOBERLY

To live "soberly" means to lead a self-controlled, disciplined life. Contrary to what some individuals believe, God's grace does not issue a license to sin. In Romans 6:1 Paul asked, "Shall we continue in sin, that grace may abound?" He quickly answered, "God forbid. How shall we, that are dead to sin, live any longer therein?" (v. 2). God's grace teaches us to practice self-control.

While training for Olympic competition, runners might enjoy seven-layered lasagna and pecan pie with ice cream, but they forego the pleasure in order to stay in shape. Similarly, the Christian who lives for God willingly refuses whatever may hinder him from winning the race set before him (Hebrews 12:1).

3. Read 1 Corinthians 9:27. What did the apostle Paul keep under control?

4. Read 1 Peter 1:13. What did Peter tell us to "gird up" and keep under control?

According to Romans 12:1 and 2, every Christian should dedicate his body and mind to God. Doing so is prerequisite to knowing "that good, and acceptable, and perfect, will of God."

The Christian's body is the temple of the Holy Spirit (1 Corinthians 6:19). We should glorify God in our body (v. 20).

Both the body and the mind are subject to impulses that may distract us from living for God. We may overindulge the body or overwork it to the neglect of our spiritual good. However, self-control treats the body as a vehicle for serving God and keeps us, therefore, from becoming lazy or burned out. Self-control also guards the mind against evil stimuli (Matthew 15:19) while allowing right thoughts (Philippians 4:8) to promote our spiritual growth.

5. What specific temptations will you refuse in order to honor the Lord with your body?

6. What specific temptations will you refuse in order to honor the Lord with your mind?

LIVE RIGHTEOUSLY

What does it mean to live righteously? It means to conduct ourselves in an upright, just manner in the sight of our fellow human beings. We should live in such a way that no one can point to any wrongdoing in us. Our actions resemble those of Jesus, Who "went about doing good" (Acts 10:38).

"Righteously" translates the Greek word dikaios, *denoting right conduct or a state of being right.*

Jesus always pleased His Heavenly Father (John 8:29). Even when Jesus was physically exhausted, hungry, and thirsty, and the Devil tempted Him severely, He refused to sin. Indeed, His entire life was sinless; therefore, not even His enemies could find any fault in Him. They resorted to false accusations and used false witnesses to level charges against Him when they clamored for His crucifixion (Matthew 26:59, 60).

7. Read Luke 23:4. What authority figure admitted he found no fault in Jesus?

8. Read 1 Peter 1:19. How did Peter describe Jesus?

The Christian's life should withstand the scrutiny of those who know him or her best. No one should be able to say legitimately, "She claims to be a Christian but refuses to pay her bills on time," or "He has a foul

Ephesians 5:8 teaches that believers have been transferred from a life of darkness to a life of light and should therefore "walk as children of light."

mouth," or "She is a lazy worker," or "He is the worst neighbor on the block."

Paul told the Christians at Philippi that he was praying they would lead an upright life (Philippians 1:9). He wanted them to be "sincere and without offence till the day of Christ" (v. 10). Later he wrote, "Do all things without murmurings and disputings: that ye may be blameless and harmless, the sons of God, without rebuke, in the midst of a crooked and perverse nation" (2:14, 15). Such a life would stand in stark contrast to their pagan neighbors' lives. The Philippian Christians would "shine as lights in the world" (v. 15).

9. Read Matthew 5:16. What is the ultimate purpose of shining as lights in the world?

LIVE GODLY

As we have seen, living righteously defines how we relate to our fellow human beings. Living godly defines how we relate to our Heavenly Father. Both relationships are crucially important to the issue of living for God.

The word translated "godly" in Titus 2:12 is *eusebos,* meaning "piously" or "reverently." A truly godly person esteems God highly. He humbles himself in God's sight, worships Him exclusively, and maintains a constant awareness of His presence.

This pious attitude springs from a sincere love of God and is the proper response to what

Jesus called "the greatest commandment." He said, "Thou shalt love the Lord thy God with all thy heart, and with all thy soul, and with all thy mind" (Matthew 22:37).

A loving marriage relationship illustrates the relationship pious believers have with God. A loving husband tries to please his wife and values her above all other human beings. His happiest moments are those he spends with her. He willingly puts her interests ahead of his own. A loving wife esteems her husband highly, acknowledges his leadership in the home, and delights in his presence. Similarly, if we love God, we value Him supremely, endeavor to please Him always, acknowledge His leadership, and delight in His presence.

Ephesians 5:22–33 describes the model marriage: husband and wife bound together in mutual love for the Lord and loving each other selflessly.

10. Read Deuteronomy 10:12 and 13. What five responsibilities should the believer honor in his or her relationship with God?

 (a)

 (b)

 (c)

 (d)

 (e)

Jesus set the perfect example of godliness. He lived from the manger to the grave in complete dedication to His Heavenly Father. He often prayed early in the morning and maintained unbroken fellowship with the

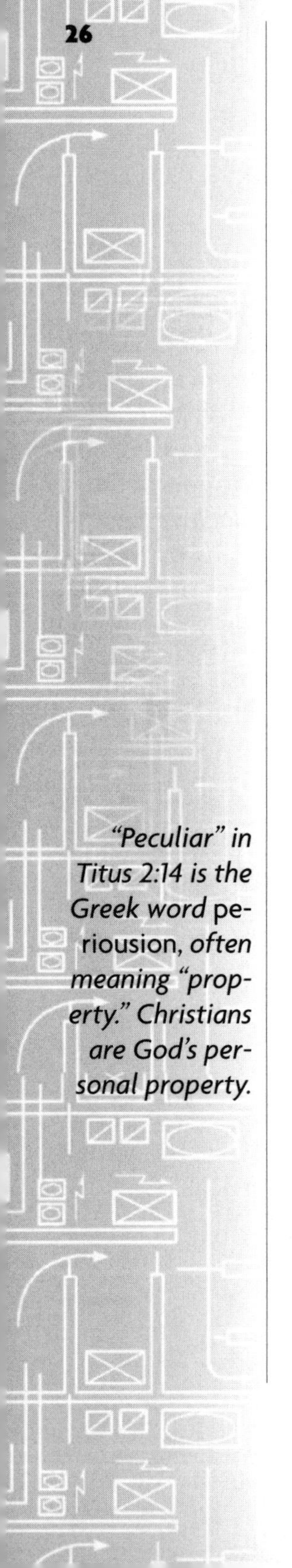

"Peculiar" in Titus 2:14 is the Greek word periousion, *often meaning "property." Christians are God's personal property.*

Father. Jesus was praying on a high mountain when the Father affirmed Jesus' dedication to Him. He announced, "This is my beloved Son, in whom I am well pleased" (Matthew 17:5; cf. Luke 9:28, 35).

Titus 2:13 and 14 offer two strong incentives to live for God. Verse 13 tells us Jesus will return. If we anticipate His return and hope for it, we will conduct our lives appropriately. We will avoid any behavior we would be ashamed of doing when He appears. We will choose to engage in faithful service to Him.

The apostle John understood the strong incentive Jesus' return provides. He wrote: "And now, little children, abide in him; that, when he shall appear, we may have confidence, and not be ashamed before him at his coming" (1 John 2:28).

Titus 2:14 discloses the second incentive to live for God. It is the incentive of knowing Christ gave Himself for us, "that he might redeem us from all iniquity, and purify unto himself a peculiar people, zealous of good works." Here, in succinct form, is a declaration of God's will for us. He wants us to be His pure, distinct people who enthusiastically perform good deeds.

Living for God, then, expresses our gratitude for Jesus' sacrifice on our behalf and embraces God's noble purpose for us.

11. Read Galatians 6:10. For whom should believers do good?

12. Read Colossians 3:22 and 23. Why should the believer do what is right without regard for human recognition?

FOR FURTHER THOUGHT

1. Why should the believer avoid defending inappropriate behavior by claiming, "Everybody does it"?

2. Read John 14:1–3. How eagerly should believers anticipate the fulfillment of Jesus' promise to come again and receive us unto Himself? What aspect of Jesus' return are you looking forward to most eagerly?

3. Paul urged the Philippian believers to lead a different lifestyle from that of their pagan neighbors. What do you see as major differences between your lifestyle and that of unsaved acquaintances?

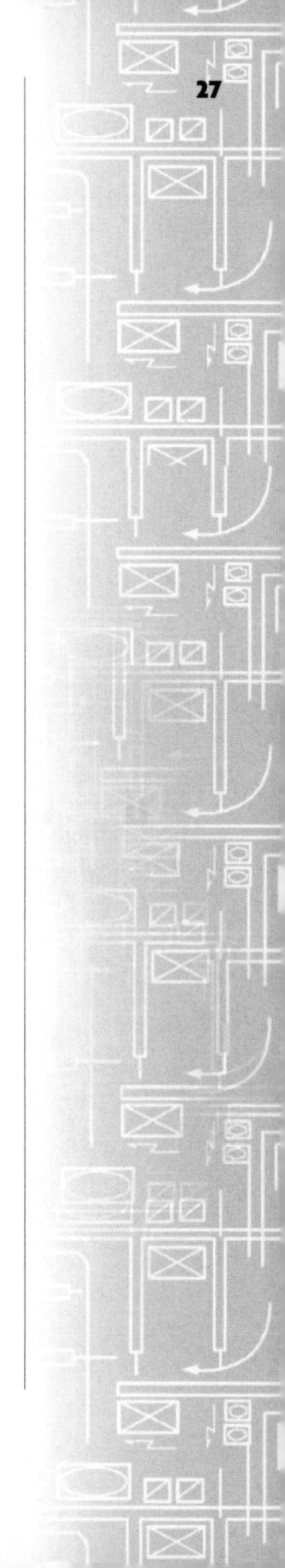

LESSON **3**

Christ Lives in You

"I am crucified with Christ: nevertheless I live; yet not I, but Christ liveth in me: and the life which I now live in the flesh I live by the faith of the Son of God, who loved me, and gave himself for me" (Galatians 2:20).

Is it unthinkable that the most powerful ruler in the world could become a permanent guest in your house? If the unthinkable occurred, how would you get your house in order? How would your guest's presence change your life?

If these questions stretch your thinking beyond all limits, consider this fact: if you are a Christian, the all-powerful Ruler of the universe has made your heart His home. That's right. Christ lives in you, and this amazing fact can revolutionize your life.

It certainly revolutionized the apostle Paul's life. Writing to the Galatians he declared, "Christ liveth in me" (Galatians 2:20). Paul opposed Christ with white-hot zeal until Christ humbled him, forgave his sins, and changed his life. In that memorable instant

When a person trusts in Christ as Savior, the Holy Spirit baptizes him (places him) into Christ. He thereby identifies the believer with Christ's death, burial, and resurrection.

on the Damascus Road, the Holy Spirit united Paul with Christ in His death, burial, and resurrection. Paul could say, "I am crucified with Christ" (v. 20), meaning Christ had taken all of Paul's sins on Himself at Calvary and paid the penalty of those sins on Paul's behalf.

Paul did not die physically when he became a believer. He said, "Nevertheless I live" (v. 20). However, his whole life changed because his sins were forgiven. From that point, he lived "by the faith of the Son of God" (v. 20).

1. Read Romans 6:1–4. What noticeable change is the result of our identification with Christ in His death, burial, and resurrection?

2. How did your life change when you trusted in Christ as Savior?

LIVE BY FAITH IN CHRIST

Neither determination nor natural ability enables us to succeed in the Christian life. Our pilgrimage to Heaven leads through daunting trials and temptations that *could* wear us down and destroy our resolve to live for God. We need to take to heart Jesus' words, "Without me ye can do nothing" (John 15:5). Contrast this statement with what Paul wrote in Philippians 4:13, "I can do all things through Christ which strengtheneth me." Paul learned to rely on the indwelling Christ to carry him through even the most desperate circumstances. As he testified in Galatians 2:20, "I live by the faith of the Son of God."

One of Paul's most harrowing trials occurred on the high seas. The Romans were transporting him to Rome to stand trial when a ferocious storm struck their ship. The situation devolved from ominous to hopeless as brutal winds and high waves pummeled the ship and inky blackness blotted the sky. Despair gripped everyone except Paul. He exuded hope and encouraged all those on board.

3. Read Acts 27:13–25.
   (a) What promise did Paul make (v. 22)?

   (b) On what did he base his promise (vv. 23, 24)?

   (c) What statement of faith did Paul make (v. 25)?

The same Lord Who delivered Paul dwells in you and stands ready to deliver you from trials and temptations. Recognize that He is with you always. He will never leave you or forsake you (Hebrews 13:5).

In Ephesians 6 Paul pulled no punches

in describing the battles we face in living for God. He counseled us to "be strong in the Lord, and in the power of his might" (v. 10). He explained that the Devil and his cohorts oppose us bitterly, but we can protect ourselves with the "armour of God" (v. 13) and use "the shield of faith" to "quench all the fiery darts of the wicked" (v. 16).

4. Read Romans 10:17. What does God use to build our faith?

5. Read Matthew 4:1–11. What did Jesus use to defeat the Devil?

6. What current trial will you overcome by relying on the Lord?

LIVE IN HOPE

Although you will never live free of trials and temptations as you live for God, you can anticipate a trouble-free future. These statements may seem contradictory, but the apparent contradiction vanishes in the light of two truths presented in Colossians. Verse 27 of chapter 1 teaches that Christ's presence in us is "the hope of glory." In verse 4 of chapter 3, Paul indicates this glory awaits the appearing of Christ in glory.

Nothing glorious characterized Jesus'

death. Crucifixion is gruesome and humiliating. But Jesus arose from the dead in a glorified body, incapable of suffering and dying, and vested with heavenly, eternal qualities. Someday He will come in the air to catch up all Christians from the earth, and then we will receive glorified bodies incapable of experiencing suffering, pain, and death. Our new bodies will be like Christ's glorious body. Philippians 3:20 and 21 give us this promise: "For our conversation [citizenship] is in heaven; from whence also we look for the Saviour, the Lord Jesus Christ: who shall change our vile body, that it may be fashioned like unto his glorious body."

Living for God is worthwhile in spite of all the trials and spiritual battles we encounter. Someday we will see Jesus. The struggles will be over and seem insignificant in light of the glory we will share with Him.

The event in which Jesus comes in the air to catch away Christians is the Rapture. First, the bodies of dead Christians will be raised and united with their spirits. Their resurrection bodies will take on a glorified condition. Then living Christians will be caught up, and their bodies will become glorified. See 1 Corinthians 15:51–53 and 1 Thessalonians 4:16 and 17.

7. Read Romans 8:18. To what are our current sufferings not worthy to be compared?

8. Read 1 Peter 1:7. When will faith tested by trials receive the Lord's approval?

The Christians at Thessalonica modeled faith under fire. When they stepped out of paganism to follow the Lord, they encountered persecution from their unsaved contemporaries. First Thessalonians 1:6 reveals that they "received the word in much affliction." But persecution only strengthened their faith, and soon people near and far were talking about it. These stalwart believers, in whom Christ had taken up residence, "turned to God from idols to serve the living and true God; and to wait for his Son from heaven" (vv. 9, 10).

Because Christ lives in you, you, too, can surmount every trial and serve the living and true God.

GIVE CHRIST THE KEYS TO YOUR LIFE

You probably do not give your house keys to an overnight guest, but you might give them to a permanent guest. Jesus abides permanently in all believers and should receive full rights to all that we are and have. We should give Him the keys to the house.

In his letter to the Ephesians, the apostle Paul prayed "that Christ may dwell in your hearts by faith" (3:17). The word "dwell" means to settle down and abide, to take up permanent abode. It indicates that Christ wants us to treat Him as more than an infrequent visitor. He wants us to treat Him as a permanent resident.

Perhaps you have visited the home of a friend or relative, only to discover in two or

three days the host or hostess is sending subtle signals that your welcome has expired.

9. What hints, subtle or not, might a host and hostess give to show a guest that his or her welcome has expired?

Would you feel slighted, disappointed, and offended if you were a guest in someone's home and the host or hostess ignored you? Wouldn't you feel unwelcome if the host or hostess pursued a lot of busy work and failed to take time to converse with you? Yet a Christian may ignore Jesus the same way. It is easy to become so busy working for the Lord that we fail to spend adequate time with Him.

10. What actions or attitudes on the part of a Christian might offend the indwelling Christ?

When Jesus stayed in the home of Mary and Martha, Mary "sat at Jesus' feet, and heard his word" (Luke 10:39), whereas "Martha was cumbered about much serving" (v. 40). Their responses to Jesus received different responses from Jesus.

11. Read Luke 10:41 and 42.
    (a) How did Jesus respond to Martha's obsession with busy activity?

A warning worth heeding: "Beware the barrenness of a busy life." An observation worth noting: "What matters is not the time we put into a task, but what we put into the time."

(b) How did Jesus respond to Mary's choice to spend quality time with Him?

12. What activities will you relinquish in order to spend quality time with Jesus?

If we truly wish to live for God, we must give Jesus free access to every room in the house—every part of our life. We should give Him access to our social life, allowing Him to guide our relationships. We should yield control of our business life, giving Him the uncontested right to manage our finances. We should acknowledge His right to control our thought life so His Word filters out unwholesome and ungodly thoughts. We should also turn our recreational life over to Him. Some current activities may demand too much of our time or money or passion.

Living for God involves far more than the time we spend in church. It involves the moments of every day and how they count for God. Ephesians 5:15 and 16 encourage us to conduct ourselves in a wise manner, looking around for opportunities to make the most of the time available to us. Colossians 4:5 makes a similar appeal, exhorting us to "walk in wisdom" toward unbelievers, "redeeming the time."

An Internet site asks a few simple questions before predicting the inquirer's time of death. Insurance companies compute rates based on a person's probable life expectancy before issuing a life insurance policy. In the final analysis, however, our lives are in the Lord's hands. No one can accurately predict how many years, months, or days we have left. We ought to live for the Lord today. None of us can predict whether we will be on earth or in Heaven tomorrow.

13. How will your determination to live for God affect your daily schedule?

FOR FURTHER THOUGHT

1. Under what circumstances does Christ take up residence in a person's life?

2. What is the difference between staying overnight and dwelling somewhere?

3. How does knowing Jesus dwells in you help you live for God?

LESSON **4**

Your Faithful Helper

"But the Comforter, which is the Holy Ghost, whom the Father will send in my name, he shall teach you all things, and bring all things to your remembrance, whatsoever I have said unto you" (John 14:26).

All the materials for a precut house arrived safely, much to the delight of the gentleman who ordered them. The company also sent a representative to guide the construction from start to finish. Everything should fit together perfectly if the builders follow the rep's guidance.

Building a godly life is impossible without the Helper, Who has come alongside you to guide you. He knows precisely how to fit all the parts of your life together so it will rest on a solid foundation—the Rock of Ages—and stand as a tribute to God's grace.

JESUS PROMISED TO SEND THE HELPER

Before He went to the cross Jesus promised, "I will pray the Father, and he shall give you another Comforter, that he may abide

"Comforter" is parakletos. *This Greek word combines the words for "called" and "alongside." In Greek culture* parakletos *applied to a legal advocate, a person called alongside to help a defendant. The word "Helper" appropriately identifies the Comforter's role.*

with you for ever; even the Spirit of truth" (John 14:16, 17). Jesus knew His disciples would blunder and fail unless the Holy Spirit came alongside to help them.

We, too, would fail to live for God if we did not have the ministry of the Holy Spirit.

1. Compare John 14:17 and Romans 8:9. What distinguishes Christians from unbelievers?

2. According to Jesus' promise in John 14:16, how long does the Holy Spirit live in believers?

HOW THE HOLY SPIRIT HELPS US

In living for God, our constant goal should be to demonstrate the godly qualities that marked Christ's life and ministry. These qualities, called "the fruit of the Spirit," appear in Galatians 5:22 and 23.

3. What character qualities are given in Galatians 5:22 and 23?

Only the Holy Spirit can produce this spiritual fruit in our lives. He does so gradually

but progressively. Paul wrote in 2 Corinthians 3:18: "But we all, with open face beholding as in a glass the glory of the Lord, are changed into the same image from glory to glory, even as by the Spirit of the Lord."

Let's examine some of the ways the Holy Spirit helps us reach Christlike spiritual maturity (Ephesians 4:13).

The Holy Spirit illumines our minds.

As we study the Bible to learn how God wants us to live, the Holy Spirit enables us to understand what we read. After all, He inspired the Scriptures and knows the meaning of every verse. First Corinthians 2:9–15 explains that God has revealed His plans to us by His Spirit. We can understand spiritual truth because we have received the Spirit.

4. Read 1 Corinthians 2:14. Why can't an unbeliever understand spiritual truth?

5. Read 1 Corinthians 2:13. What does the Spirit's teaching far exceed?

The Holy Spirit guides us.

Obeying God should be high on every Christian's list of priorities. We cannot live for God and be godly unless we do what He wants us to do. It is not always easy to know God's will, but the Holy Spirit faithfully guides us.

Acts 16:6–10 reports that twice the Holy

The Holy Spirit never leads us to do anything that contradicts Scripture. He is "the Spirit of truth" and always leads us "into all truth" (John 16:13).

Spirit refused to let Paul and his coworkers go where they planned. He intervened somehow to move them in the direction God wanted them to take. Similarly, the Holy Spirit may close some doors and open others so we will serve God where He chooses. He may bring a relevant passage of Scripture to our attention, or He may use circumstances, or He may lead us to a mature Christian for wise counsel.

The Holy Spirit helps us to pray.

We cannot live for God effectively unless we pray. Just as soldiers need to communicate with their base of operations for direction and supplies, so we need to communicate with our Heavenly Father. Our effectiveness on the front lines of Christian service depends on prayer. We may not always know how to pray in a given situation or even how to express our deepest desires, but the Holy Spirit intercedes for us. Romans 8:26 assures us that the Spirit makes "intercession for us with groanings which cannot be uttered."

Ephesians 6:18 commands us to pray "always with all prayer and supplication in the Spirit."

The Holy Spirit equips us.

It would be impossible to live for God if we did not have the Holy Spirit's enabling. He has equipped every Christian with all that he or she needs to live for God. The New Testament identifies an array of gifts endowed upon us by the Spirit.

6. Read Romans 5:5.
   (a) What has the Holy Spirit placed in our hearts?

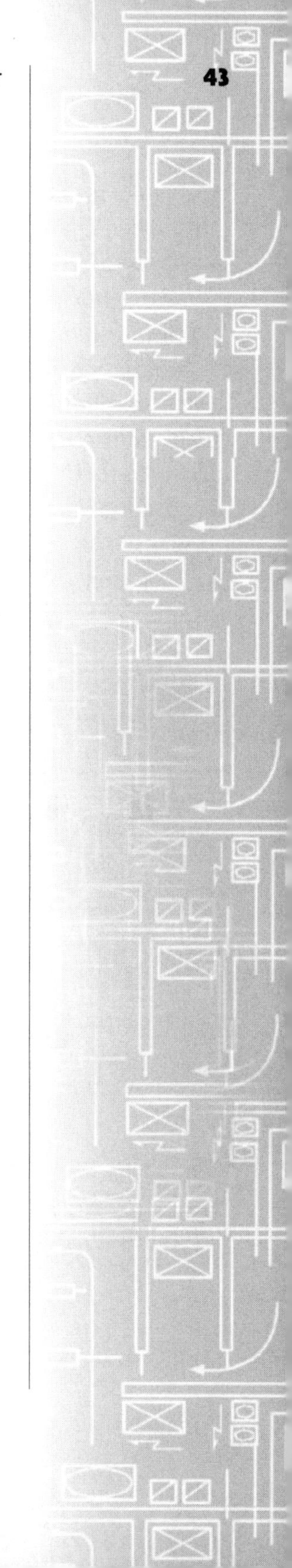

(b) How has this gift affected your relationship with God?

(c) How has this gift affected your relationship with others?

Before the New Testament was fully written, the Holy Spirit equipped certain believers, notably the apostles, with sign gifts. These temporary gifts helped persuade unbelievers that the gospel is truly God's message. Eventually, as more and more of the New Testament became available, the sign gifts faded away. They were the gift of apostleship (1 Corinthians 12:28), the gift of prophecy (v. 28), the gift of wisdom and knowledge (v. 8), the gift of faith (v. 9), the gift of healing (v. 9), the gift of miracles (v. 10), the gift of discerning spirits (v. 10), the gift of tongues (v. 10), and the gift of interpretation (v. 10).

Other gifts imparted by the Holy Spirit are permanent and manifested today by faithful believers.

7. Read Ephesians 4:11 and 12. What purposes do spiritual gifts serve?

8. Read Romans 12:6–8 and Ephesians 4:11. What spiritual gifts did Paul list in these passages?

Some Bible teachers suggest the gift of prophecy (Romans 12:6) and the gift of "prophets" (Ephesians 4:11) refer to forth-telling and preachers.

9. Which spiritual gift(s) do you believe the Spirit has given you?

The Holy Spirit exercises His sovereign will in the distribution of spiritual gifts. First Corinthians 12:11 credits Him with "dividing to every man severally as he will." Every gift, whether prominent or not, is necessary and serves a significant purpose in the care and growth of the Body of Christ (vv. 20–27).

The Holy Spirit fills us.

Paul commanded the Christians at Ephesus to "be filled with the Spirit" (Ephesians 5:18). The verb "be filled" indicates continuous action. Therefore, we must not think of the filling with the Spirit as a one-time crisis experience that instantly transforms us into victorious Christians. The Christian life is a journey, not a single step. To live for God as godly believers, we must constantly avail ourselves of the Spirit's enabling.

The concept of being continuously filled with the Spirit should be understood as being continuously controlled by the Spirit. Ephesians 5:18 contrasts this experience with that of being drunk. Just as a drunk person is "under the influence" of alcohol, so the Spirit-filled believer is under the influence of the Spirit. The Spirit influences or controls his life, causing him to humbly fulfill God's role for him.

10. Scan Ephesians 5:18—6:6. What three

walks of life are positively affected when a believer is filled with (controlled by) the Spirit?

HOW WE COOPERATE WITH THE HOLY SPIRIT

We must not take the enabling ministry of the Holy Spirit for granted. If we do, our lives will be barren, ineffective, and unfulfilling. However, if we cooperate with the Holy Spirit as He ministers in and through us, our lives will be fruitful, effective, and fulfilling.

We must not lie to the Holy Spirit.

Acts 5 presents the tragic account of a husband and wife who lied to the Holy Spirit by pretending to give to their local church all the funds they had received from a property transaction. Their lie cost them their lives.

Lying to the Holy Spirit is a serious sin, whether it carries a death sentence or not. It certainly withholds God's blessing and tarnishes our testimony. Perhaps hypocrisy is the most common form of lying to the Holy Spirit. Too often we pretend to be dedicated to the Lord. We may sing about our devotion to Jesus while refusing to obey Him. We may talk about our love for the lost while refusing to share the gospel with our neighbors. We may sing, "All to Jesus I Surrender," while refusing to give Him a respectful offering.

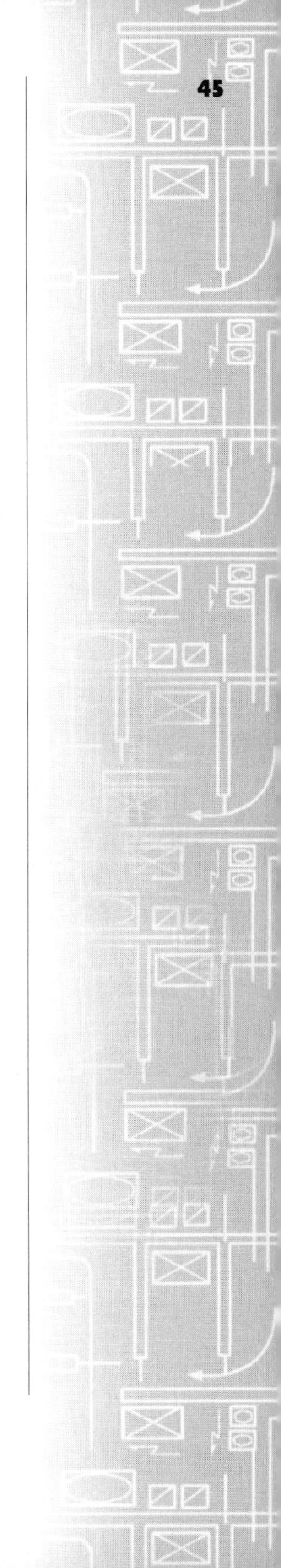

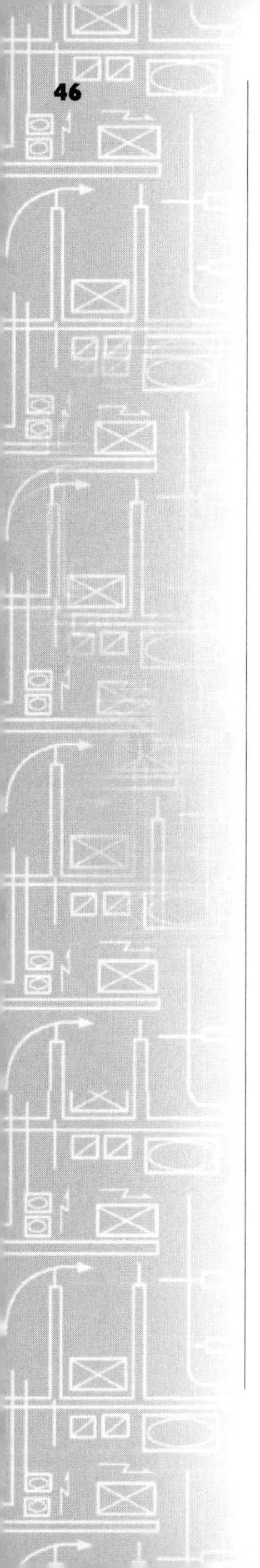

We may sing, "There Is Joy in Serving Jesus," while refusing to assume any ministry in the local church.

11. Read Psalm 139:23 and 24. What prayer serves as a model for us if we wish to be honest in our relationship with the Holy Spirit?

We must not grieve the Holy Spirit.

The Holy Spirit changes us gradually into the image of Christ (2 Corinthians 3:18), but we may hinder this gracious ministry and thereby grieve the Spirit.

12. Read Ephesians 4:30. What command did Paul issue?

We grieve the Holy Spirit by sinning, because sin hinders His ministry of making us Christlike. Just as a disobedient child grieves his or her parent, so we grieve the Holy Spirit when we disobey our Heavenly Father.

13. Read 1 John 1:9. What should we do when we grieve the Holy Spirit by sinning?

We must not quench the Holy Spirit.

The Holy Spirit prompts us to be all that God wants us to be and to do all that God wants us to do. He ignites a zeal for righteousness in us and stirs in us the fervor to love God and others. Romans 5:5 tells us the Holy Spirit has shed the love of God in our hearts, and 1 Peter 1:22 exhorts us to love our brothers in Christ without hypocrisy and "with a pure heart fervently." First Peter 1:22 links this duty with the ministry of the Spirit. If we stifle this zeal and fervor, we disobey the clear command in 1 Thessalonians 5:19, "Quench not the Spirit."

14. What do you believe the Holy Spirit is prompting you to do?

15. How will you cooperate with Him and not quench Him?

The church's first martyr, Stephen, accused the Jewish nation of persistently resisting the Holy Spirit (Acts 7:51). Hebrews 10:29 mentions the possibility of doing "despite unto the Spirit of grace." This verse indicates it is possible to insult Him.

FOR FURTHER THOUGHT

1. What does it mean to you personally that the Holy Spirit resides permanently in you?

2. The Holy Spirit is a Person, not a power or influence. How should this truth impact your relationship with Him?

3. Scan Colossians 3:16—4:1. How does this passage harmonize with Ephesians 5:18—6:6? What link do you see between the role of the Spirit and the Scriptures?

LESSON **5**

Daily Resources for Living for God

"Thy word is a lamp unto my feet, and a light unto my path" (Psalm 119:105).

When it comes to food, some people can really pack it away. If you need proof, visit an all-you-can-eat buffet and notice the mountains of food some patrons pile on their plates. Eating can be a broadening experience, especially for those who do not eat to live but live to eat.

Of course, a healthy physical appetite controlled by sensible eating habits and accompanied by daily exercise helps to energize us and promote optimal cell growth. Similarly, God has provided daily resources for our optimal spiritual health. The Scriptures are bread for the soul, and prayer is exercise for the soul. When we avail ourselves of these essential resources, we grow strong spiritually and are well equipped to serve Him. The words

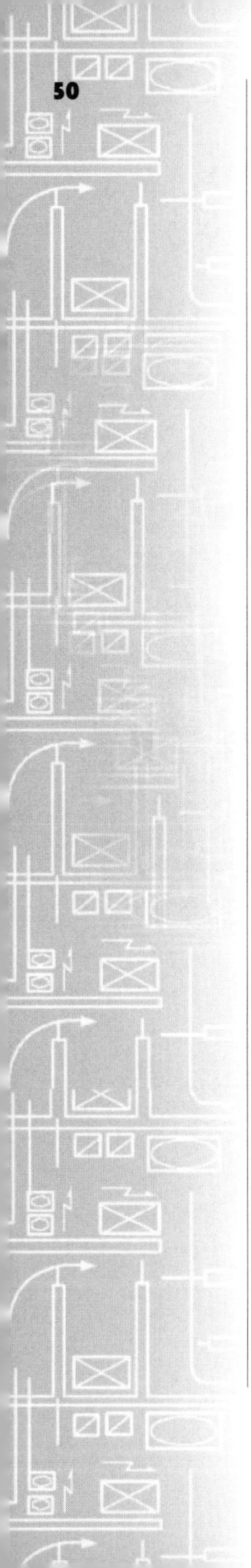

of a children's Sunday School chorus may be simple, but the message is profound: "Read your Bible, pray every day, and you'll grow, grow, grow."

THE RESOURCE OF SCRIPTURE

When the Devil tempted Jesus to command stones to become bread, Jesus quoted Deuteronomy 8:3, "Man doth not live by bread only, but by every word that proceedeth out of the mouth of the LORD" (see Matthew 4:4). Although Jesus was hungry, He valued obedience to God's Word far above satisfying His hunger.

To lead a godly life—to live for God—we need to value God's Word. Just as Jesus quoted Scripture to ward off Satan's temptations, we need to know Scripture well enough to apply it to the temptations we face. For example, if Satan tempts us to honor something or someone above God, we should be able to apply the command, "Thou shalt have no other gods before me" (Exodus 20:3) to that situation. If he tempts us to steal, we should be able to recall the command, "Thou shalt not steal" (v. 15).

1. Read Ephesians 6:11–17. What offensive weapon did Paul command us to use in battling the Devil and his followers?

2. How much Scripture do you know by heart?

   ____ None

____ Very little

____ A fair amount

____ A lot

You cannot read the Bible without recognizing that God extends His love to the whole wide world. John 3:16, perhaps the most memorized verse in the Bible, broadcasts God's love. God so loved the world that He gave His Son, Jesus, to provide salvation for sinners. All who respond to God's love by believing in Jesus escape perdition and receive everlasting life.

But John 3:16 and Acts 1:8 connect to each other. As recipients of God's love and everlasting life, we bear responsibility to be Jesus' witnesses. As Acts 1:8 indicates, we must pass along the good news of Jesus "unto the uttermost part of the earth." To fulfill this responsibility we must share God's Word generously. Unless we do so, we cannot claim to be living for God.

3. Read Psalm 119:130. What does the Word of God accomplish?

4. Read Psalm 19:7. What else does God's Word accomplish?

5. Read 2 Timothy 3:15. What do the Scriptures accomplish?

6. Read Romans 10:14. What do unbelievers need to connect with God's good news?

7. Read Mark 16:15. What do you see as your obligation if you desire to live for God?

As we share God's Word, it falls on various kinds of soil (see Mark 4:14–20). Some to whom we witness reject it; others ignore it; but some receive it and become spiritually productive. We cannot give life to unbelievers, but we can share "the word of life" with them. For this reason Paul encouraged the Philippian Christians to "[hold] forth the word of life" (Philippians 2:16).

8. Read 1 Peter 1:23–25.
   (a) What part does Scripture play in the new birth (v. 23)?

   (b) How long will God's Word remain (v. 23)?

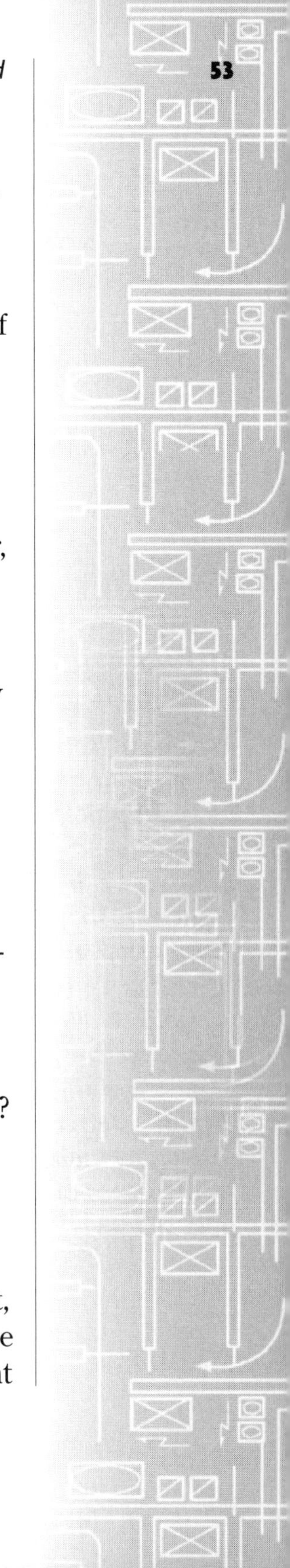

(c) What did the apostles and early Christians proclaim (v. 25)?

God's Word serves as a constant source of nourishment for our spiritual life. We cannot become godly and live for God without making it our daily sustenance. The hunger of the five thousand who feasted on the bread and fish Jesus multiplied was fully satisfied. John 6:12 reports they were "filled." Later, however, Jesus emphasized the far greater importance of being filled with His words. He said, "It is the spirit that quickeneth; the flesh profiteth nothing: the words that I speak unto you, they are spirit, and they are life" (v. 63).

The apostle Peter understood the need to feast on God's Word. He urged, "As newborn babes, desire the sincere milk of the word, that ye may grow thereby" (1 Peter 2:2). A baby cannot grow properly without milk, nor can a newborn Christian grow spiritually without drinking the milk of the Word.

9. Read Psalm 119:103. To what does this verse compare God's words? What does this comparison suggest about Bible study?

Have you watched a cow eat silage or grass? If you have, you know the cow chews it, chews it again, and chews it again. That bovine eating habit serves as a model for all who want to lead a godly life. We must read God's Word thoughtfully, "chewing on" its truth slowly and repeatedly.

Psalm 1 recommends this slow, deliberate masticating of Scripture. It affirms that the man who delights in and meditates on God's Word "day and night" is "blessed" (happy, spiritually prosperous). This psalm also affirms that such a man grows spiritually and becomes productive.

10. Read Psalm 1:3. What does the person resemble as he delights in God's Word and meditates on it?

Psalm 19:10 sets a high value on the Scriptures by announcing, "More to be desired are they than gold, yea, than much fine gold." Psalm 119:72 declares, "The law of thy mouth is better unto me than thousands of gold and silver."

It takes time to familiarize yourself with God's Word, but it also requires a plan—a systematic way to mine its gold nuggets. Some Christians enjoy reading the entire Bible every year. Some focus on an analytical study of one book of the Bible at a time. Others prefer a topical form of Bible study, tracing, for example, what the Bible teaches about salvation, God, or Heaven. Still others like to study Bible characters. You may prefer the following devotional method before branching into other forms of Bible study.

This method works best by reading through a book of the Bible and selecting one passage (perhaps a chapter or two or three paragraphs) at a time. You simply follow the ABCs and write down your findings and questions.

Take, for example, Ephesians 1:1–23. Look for the following:

- Any prayers to echo
- Blessings to claim
- Commands to obey
- Difficulties to investigate
- Examples to follow
- Failures to avoid

As you meditate upon a passage of Scripture, keep in mind that God uses His Word to mature you and equip you for His service.

11. Read 2 Timothy 3:16. What four purposes does the Bible serve?

THE RESOURCE OF PRAYER

Prayer and Bible study complement each other. God speaks to us through the Bible, and we speak to God in prayer. Prayer helps us lead a life that honors God. Without prayer, we will fall to temptation and get crushed by trials. As someone remarked, "Seven days without prayer makes one weak." On the other hand, we are strong when we are on our knees.

It seems King David was most fervent not in his royal palace, but in the caves and ravines of the wilderness. Hunted by those who wanted to kill him, David cast himself upon

the Lord. Many psalms record his prayers. For example, in Psalm 54 he cried, "Hear my prayer, O God; give ear to the words of my mouth. For strangers are risen up against me, and oppressors seek after my soul" (vv. 2, 3).

We, too, face hard circumstances and harsh enemies, but when we are flat on our back we can look up, pray, and cast ourselves upon God. God has promised, "Call upon me in the day of trouble: I will deliver thee, and thou shalt glorify me" (Psalm 50:15).

"Supplication" in Philippians 4:6 suggests strong, urgent pleading.

Paul, who lived for God in spite of many trials, wrote from prison to encourage us to pray with thanksgiving (Philippians 4:6). He reminds us that "the peace of God, which passeth all understanding, shall keep your hearts and minds through Christ Jesus" (v. 7).

The prophet Daniel lived for God. Although the Babylonians had taken him from his Hebrew homeland to pagan Babylon, they could not take away his love for God. Surrounded by pagan deities, Daniel prayed faithfully to the living God. Even under threat of execution, he prayed. God responded to his prayers by preserving him in the lions' den and glorifying Himself through the episode.

12. Scan Daniel 6:1–11.

    (a) What trap did Daniel's adversaries set?

    (b) Did Daniel know about the decree?

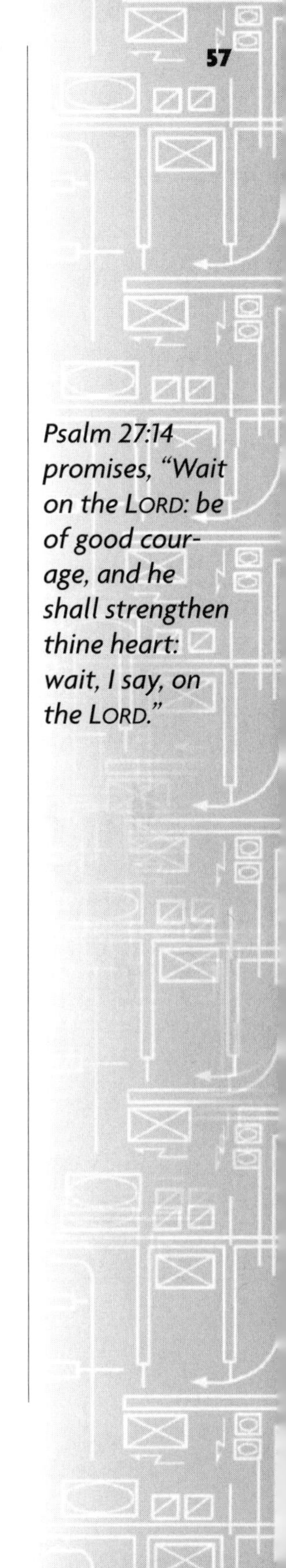

(c) What course of action did Daniel take?

(d) What course of action would you have taken?

Prayer establishes a close relationship—an intimate fellowship—with our Heavenly Father. As we spend time with Him in prayer, we become better prepared to face life with a triumphant attitude. We learn to "rest in the LORD, and wait patiently for him" (Psalm 37:7). His desires become our desires.

Psalm 27:14 promises, "Wait on the LORD: be of good courage, and he shall strengthen thine heart: wait, I say, on the LORD."

No unselfish request goes unheard when we call on the Lord in prayer. Whatever concerns us concerns our Lord. Further, nothing is too hard for Him to handle. He sympathizes with our burdens and "was in all points tempted like as we are, yet without sin" (Hebrews 4:15). Therefore, He invites us to "come boldly unto the throne of grace" (v. 16).

13. According to Hebrews 4:16, what do we obtain by going boldly to the throne of grace?

14. What concerns will you take to the Lord in prayer?

FOR FURTHER THOUGHT

1. Prayer is essential to a life that honors God. Why not spend ten minutes today telling God why you love Him?

2. Try to memorize one verse a day from each chapter in the Gospel of John. In just twenty-one days, you will have memorized one verse from each chapter.

3. Read Psalm 119 in its entirety this week.

LESSON **6**

Maintain an Attitude of Gratitude

"Oh that men would praise the LORD for his goodness, and for his wonderful works to the children of men!" (Psalm 107:8).

Conscientious parents train their children to say thank you. From the time a child is old enough to speak, a father or mother asks, "Did you say thank you?" Giving thanks should be a normal part of daily living not only in childhood but also in adulthood.

As Psalm 107:8 points out, human beings should praise the Lord for His wonderful works on their behalf. Thanksgiving Day in America was established for this specific purpose, but many individuals and families observe it as "Turkey Day." Instead of offering gratitude, they opt for gluttony and ignore the Giver of "every good gift and every perfect gift" (James 1:17).

Old Testament animal sacrifices included the burnt offering (see Leviticus 1:1–17). The voluntary offering showed the presenter's devotion to God (v. 3). The animal was cut into pieces, laid on the altar, and burned (v. 12). The entire sacrifice was consumed, symbolizing complete submission to God. In like manner, believers should present every part of their lives to God as a sacrifice. They should offer their entire lives to God.

1. What are some benefits the Lord has bestowed on all human beings?

2. Read Acts 17:28. What universal blessings did the apostle Paul attribute to God in his address to the Athenians?

Christians ought to stand out in twenty-first century culture as those who acknowledge God's goodness and praise Him with thankful hearts. Indeed, a proper appreciation of His goodness persuades us to live for Him. Thanksgiving leads to "thanksliving."

OUR THANK-YOU GIFT TO GOD

The "mercies of God" provide sufficient reason to present our bodies as "a living sacrifice, holy, acceptable unto God" (Romans 12:1). The word "mercies" means "compassion." God has been profoundly good to us by lavishing His compassion on us. Although we were lost sinners, He loved us and made it possible for us to be saved and enjoy all the benefits of His grace.

3. Read the following verses. What are some compassionate deeds God has lavished on us?
   (a) Romans 3:24

   (b) Romans 4:7

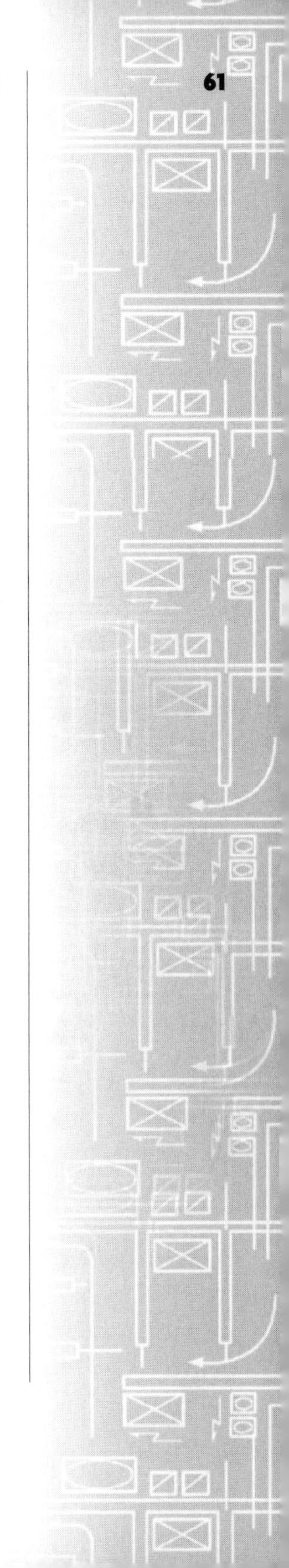

(c) Romans 5:1 and 2

(d) Romans 5:9

(e) Romans 5:11

(f) Romans 6:5

(g) Romans 6:18

(h) Romans 8:14

(i) Romans 8:35

Giving God our bodies is an act of thanksgiving, but this act should also include offering Him our minds. Paul counseled us to avoid the kind of thinking that characterizes the evil world system. As our minds undergo renewal, we will "prove what is that good, and acceptable, and perfect, will of God" (Romans 12:2).

What we think affects how we act. If we fill our minds with evil thoughts, our actions will be evil. Proverbs 23:7 teaches, "For as he thinketh in his heart, so is he." Living for God demands a pure thought life.

4. Read Philippians 4:8. What things should the believer think on?

Evil philosophies of life vie for attention, but only a Biblical philosophy will fuel an attitude of gratitude. The world says man can get along fine without God. It tries to dethrone God and crown mankind the supreme ruler. It argues that mankind deserves the credit for every achievement. It claims mankind can solve every problem and build a utopian society. However, a Biblical philosophy acknowledges man's inability to tame the sin nature, solve his problems, establish peace, and build a heaven on earth. Only a Biblical view of life leads us to understand how much we owe to God and how appropriate it is to praise Him.

5. Read Genesis 6:5. What did God perceive to be the thoughts of the human race before the Flood?

Jesus affirmed the law's teaching that we must love the Lord our God "with all thy mind" (Luke 10:27).

6. Read 2 Corinthians 10:5. What should Christians do about harmful thoughts?

7. What are a few harmful philosophies shaping modern culture?

GRUMBLING DISPLEASES THE LORD

Godliness and grumbling are poles apart. A chronic grumbler sees only thorns on a rose bush. He pities himself as he encounters hardships. As a result, he allows his trials to come between him and the Lord. In this dismal emotional state, he expends valuable energy licking his wounds instead of living for God.

When the Israelites journeyed through the wilderness, they saw only thorns. They interpreted their hunger to mean the Lord was unfair. They grumbled and asked whether the Lord had extricated them from Egypt only to snuff out their lives in the wilderness (Exodus 16:2, 3). Although the Lord expressed displeasure with the grumbling, He graciously and miraculously provided an abundant supply of food.

8. Read Exodus 16:13–15. What did the Lord provide to alleviate the Israelites' hunger?

This grumbling became a pattern that Hebrews 3:7–11 recalls as a serious offense against the Lord and one that Christians must not commit (v. 12). When trials bombard us, we should see them as tools that refine our character (Romans 8:18–28), prove the genuineness of our faith (1 Peter 1:7), and motivate us to pray (Philippians 4:6, 7; Hebrews 4:14–16). Instead of holding a pity party, we can praise the Lord for His help in the past and trust Him to bring us through our present struggles. We can trust Him to use our trials to make us better, not bitter.

Romans 8 highlights the role of trials in shaping believers into the image of Christ. They are an essential part of the all things that "work together for good to them that love God, to them who are the called according to his purpose" (v. 28).

Job stands out in Scripture as someone who experienced numerous trials. He lost his children, his livestock, and his health, but he did not lose his faith. He declared, "Though

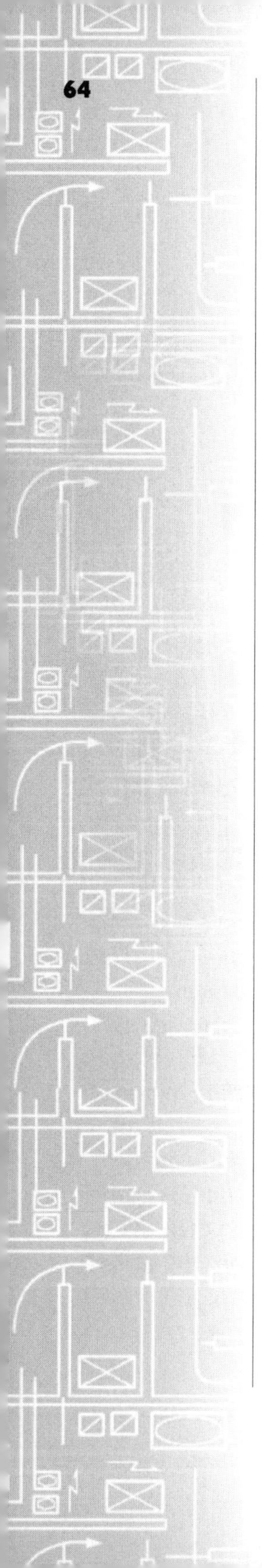

[the Lord] slay me, yet will I trust in him: but I will maintain mine own ways before him. He also shall be my salvation." (Job 13:15, 16).

The apostle Paul, too, refused to let affliction dampen his confidence in the Lord. Three times he asked the Lord to remove "a thorn in the flesh" (2 Corinthians 12:7, 8). However, the Lord refused Paul's request, choosing instead to place His grace alongside the thorn. He told Paul, "My grace is sufficient for thee: for my strength is made perfect in weakness" (v. 9). Through this unidentified affliction, Paul drew closer to the Lord and found the Lord's power resting upon him (vv. 9, 10).

9. According to Romans 5:3, what important quality do tribulations produce in us?

10. Read 1 Thessalonians 5:18. What exhortation did Paul give?

11. What trial are you experiencing? Can you thank God for it?

GRATITUDE PLEASES GOD

Just as a loving parent feels glad when his children say thank you instead of complaining, so the Lord enjoys the praises of His people. Psalm 50:14 directs us to "offer unto God

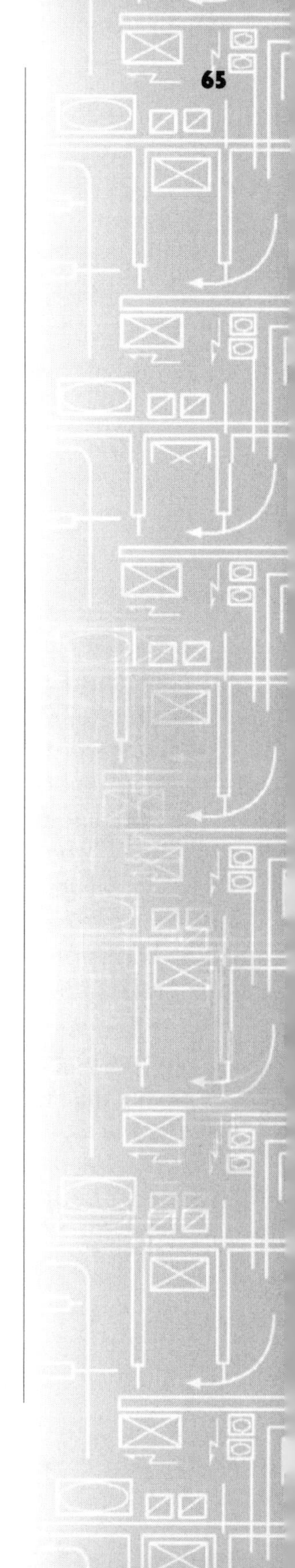

thanksgiving." Verse 23 declares, "Whoso offereth praise glorifieth me."

As we live for God, we should offer Him not only our petitions but also our praises. Making a list of reasons we are thankful may jump-start a personal litany of praise. As the hymn writer advised, "Count your many blessings, name them one by one, / And it will surprise you what the Lord hath done."

The book of Psalms includes many praises to the Lord. By reading what the psalmists declared about Him, we gain a deeper appreciation of Him and His works.

12. Read these verses from Psalms and write a characteristic or deed for which you should praise the Lord.
    (a) Psalm 7:17

    (b) Psalm 28:6, 7

    (c) Psalm 30:4

    (d) Psalm 63:3, 4

    (e) Psalm 89:5

    (f) Psalm 96:2–4

    (g) Psalm 100:4, 5

    (h) Psalm 139:14

    (i) Psalm 147:5

We often consider first-century believers examples of what it means to live for God. They witnessed faithfully, maintained unity, and prayed fervently. But they also expressed heartfelt gratitude to God. In spite of persecution and other hardships, they praised the Lord. Acts 2:47 reports that after the Day of Pentecost, the believers at Jerusalem "[praised] God." That same spirit of gratitude marked Paul's life and ministry. He greeted the Ephesians by stating, "Blessed be the God and Father of our Lord Jesus Christ" (1:3). In verse 20 of chapter 3 he burst into spontaneous praise, and near the end of the letter he encouraged the Ephesians to "[sing and make] melody in [their] heart to the Lord" (5:19).

The word "blessed" in Ephesians 1:3 translates a Greek word made up of eu, *meaning "well," and* logeo, *meaning "speak." The exhortation, "Blessed be the God and Father" suggests, "Speak well of the God and Father of our Lord Jesus Christ."*

The Christian should offer a melody of praise to the Lord daily and also write a melody of praise across the pages of his life.

FOR FURTHER THOUGHT

1. Read Ephesians 5:18–20 and notice how the giving of thanks is related to being filled with the Holy Spirit. What does this association tell you about the person who lives for God?

2. David wrote many psalms of praise when he was undergoing severe trials. Why not use one of your trials as an occasion to write a psalm of praise to God?

3. Read Revelation 5:9–14. This passage describes a future scene in Heaven. What important act of worship does this passage identify?

Wrap-up

After challenging the Christians at Thessalonica to live for God, the apostle Paul closed his first letter to them with powerful encouragement. He wrote, "And the very God of peace sanctify you wholly; and I pray God your whole spirit and soul and body be preserved blameless unto the coming of our Lord Jesus Christ" (1 Thessalonians 5:23).

The responsibility of living for God does not rest solely on your shoulders. God partners with you. He will strengthen and equip you for every good work—"unto the coming of our Lord Jesus Christ."

May you seize every opportunity He gives to "let your light so shine before men, that they may see your good works, and glorify your Father which is in heaven" (Matthew 5:16).

Answers

LESSON 1

1. Because the Lord had chosen Israel, protected her, and brought her into the Promised Land.
2. Personal answers.
3. The people chose to serve and obey the Lord.
4. (a) He said that they had fished all night and had caught nothing. (b) To obey the Lord. (c) A great reward, a miraculous catch of fish.
5. To forsake all and follow Jesus.
6. (a) The risen Lord. (b) He must have feared the risen Lord would slay him. (c) He was willing to do whatever the Lord commanded.
7. Personal answers.
8. Personal answers.
9. Answers will vary.
10. Personal answers.
11. Personal answers.
12. The palace, Caesar's household, and all other places.

LESSON 2

1. He will meet all our needs.
2. To work in our lives to fulfill His will for us.
3. His body.
4. Our minds.
5. Personal answers.
6. Personal answers.
7. Pilate.
8. As "a lamb without blemish and without spot."
9. To bring glory to God.

10. (a) To fear Him. (b) To walk in all His ways. (c) To love Him. (d) To serve Him with all his or her heart and with all his or her soul. (e) To keep His commandments.

11. All men, but especially believers.

12. The Lord will reward the believer for doing right; the believer serves the Lord, not men.

LESSON 3

1. The believer no longer lives in sin; he walks in newness of life.

2. Personal answers.

3. (a) No life would be lost. (b) The angel's assurance that God would spare everyone. (c) "Sirs, I believe God."

4. The Word of God.

5. The Scriptures.

6. Personal answers.

7. The glory that will be revealed in us.

8. At Jesus' appearing.

9. Answers will vary.

10. Answers will vary.

11. (a) He gently rebuked her. (b) He commended her.

12. Personal answers.

13. Personal answers.

LESSON 4

1. The Holy Spirit lives in believers but not in unbelievers.

2. Forever.

3. Love, joy, peace, longsuffering, gentleness, goodness, faith, meekness, and temperance (self-control).

4. Truth is spiritually discerned.

5. Human wisdom.

6. (a) The love of God. (b), (c) Personal answers.

7. The perfecting of the saints, the work of the ministry, the edifying of the body of Christ.

8. Prophecy, ministry, teaching, exhortation, giving, ruling (administration), mercy, apostles, prophets, evangelists, pastors, and teachers.

9. Personal answers.

10. Church, home, workplace.

11. "Search me, O God, and know my heart: try me, and know my thoughts: and see if there be any wicked way in me, and lead me in the way everlasting."

12. "Grieve not the holy Spirit."

13. Confess our sins.

14. Personal answers.

15. Personal answers.

LESSON 5

1. The Sword of the Spirit (the Word of God).

2. Personal answers.

3. It gives light and understanding.

4. It converts the soul and makes the simple wise.

5. They make one wise unto salvation.

6. A preacher (someone who tells the good news of Jesus).

7. To go and help present the gospel to every creature.

8. (a) It acts as a seed that brings forth new life. (b) Forever. (c) The gospel.

9. Honey. Bible study is pleasant.

10. A tree planted by the rivers of water.

11. Doctrine, reproof, correction, and instruction in righteousness.

12. (a) They gained the king's approval to prohibit anyone from making a request of anyone other than the king

for thirty days. (b) Yes. (c) He prayed as usual. (d) Personal answers.

13. Mercy and grace to help in time of need.

14. Personal answers.

LESSON 6

1. Answers will vary (physical life, food, clothing, shelter, a beautiful environment, etc.).

2. Physical existence and sustenance.

3. (a) Justification, redemption. (b) Forgiveness. (c) peace, access, joy, hope. (d) Deliverance from wrath. (e) Joy, atonement. (f) Union with Christ. (g) Freedom from sin. (h) The Spirit's leading. (i) God's inseparable love.

4. Things that are true, honest, just, pure, lovely, of good report, of virtue, of praise.

5. Evil continually.

6. Bring them into captivity to Christ.

7. Answers will vary (humanism, atheism, evolution, pluralism, relativism, etc.).

8. Quails and manna.

9. Patience.

10. "In every thing give thanks."

11. Personal answers.

12. (a) His righteousness. (b) Answered prayer; His strength and protection. (c) His holiness. (d) His lovingkindness. (e) His faithfulness. (f) His salvation, glory, and greatness. (g) His goodness and everlasting mercy; His truth that endures to all generations. (h) His great works ("fearfully and wonderfully made"). (i) His great power; His infinite understanding.